Benazir Marjan has completed her Bachelor of Business Administration and Masters of Business Administration from United International University, Bangladesh. She has also obtained a second Master's in Applied English Language and Linguistics from the University of Liberal Arts, Bangladesh. The author intends to provide quality writing that she can publish here to enhance her career opportunities in the writing world. She is a multifaceted individual with diverse interests and perspectives.

The entire book is dedicated to my beloved mother, Nasreen Jahan, who is the only inspiration of my life.

Benazir Marjan

HOW TO INVEST IN THE STOCK MARKET CAREFULLY

AUSTIN MACAULEY PUBLISHERS™

LONDON · CAMBRIDGE · NEW YORK · SHARJAH

Copyright © Benazir Marjan 2023

All rights reserved. No part of this publication may be reproduced, distributed, or transmitted in any form or by any means, including photocopying, recording, or other electronic or mechanical methods, without the prior written permission of the publisher, except in the case of brief quotations embodied in critical reviews and certain other non-commercial uses permitted by copyright law. For permission requests, write to the publisher.

Any person who commits any unauthorized act in relation to this publication may be liable to criminal prosecution and civil claims for damages.

Ordering Information
Quantity sales: Special discounts are available on quantity purchases by corporations, associations, and others. For details, contact the publisher at the address below.

Publisher's Cataloging-in-Publication data
Marjan, Benazir
How to Invest in the Stock Market Carefully

ISBN 9781638297499 (Paperback)
ISBN 9781638297505 (ePub e-book)

Library of Congress Control Number: 2023911000

www.austinmacauley.com/us

First Published 2023
Austin Macauley Publishers LLC
40 Wall Street, 33rd Floor, Suite 3302
New York, NY 10005
USA

mail-usa@austinmacauley.com
+1 (646) 5125767

I would like to convey my jovial gratitude to Austin Macauley Publishers, USA (New York) for their assistance in the book reaching to its publication.

Next, I would like to give thanks to my parents whose enormous efforts and struggle made it happen; thus I was able to write the manuscript of my book.

Last, but not the least, I am grateful to my husband, Muttabiur Raihan SK, who gave me unconditional support to reach my goal.

1. How to Invest in Stock Market Carefully?

Category: Personal finance > Investing in stocks, bonds, real estate, and more.

Summary: Stock Market can be a good source of your income if you really understand it well. Look at the parameters, those you must consider before making any investment there.

Body: People can establish share business besides continuing their jobs as well. You just need to study, gather knowledge, and always get in touch with the index. If you have enough courage and interest, only then can you enter here. Otherwise, never start your investment by following others blindly. It may destroy your capital. At first, you need to investigate properly about the company history and go through their annual reports extensively. My suggestion is, even after investment, use your own understanding to buy and sell. One day you will be a successful trader there.

There could be two kinds of investments: long-term investment and short-term investment.

In long-term investment, you should invest in expensive companies, those that are very well renowned and established in the country. You will get cash dividends and stock dividends after one accounting year. Again, your number of shares will also increase if a stock split takes place. A stock split is a corporate action in which a company divides its existing shares into multiple shares. Basically, companies choose to split their shares, so they can lower the trading price of their stock to a range deemed comfortable by most investors and increase the liquidity of shares.

After a split, the stock price will be reduced. In the example of a 2-for-1 split, the share price will be halved. Although the number of outstanding shares increases and the price of each share changes, the company's market capitalization remains unchanged. It is a good sign for long-term investors as they won't trade immediately. The number of their shares will increase. Slowly, the price of the shares will also increase as time goes on. Therefore, they will have an increased number of shares with increased prices with time. This strategy is only for long-term investment.

In short-term investment, people buy and sell shares on a daily basis to make profit. Yes, it is quite risky. But we know if there is no risk, then there is no possibility of gain at all. Initially, you have to consider these three facts:

1. You have to analyze the last 200 days' price of a particular share. If the price is upward sloping then you can think to make a trade of that stock.

2. Try to understand the overall cycle or pattern. Since 1950, most of the stock market gains have occurred in the November to April time frame, while during the May to October period, the averages have been relatively static. As a trader, keep this pattern in your mind while making your short-term investments.
3. Try to get a sense of market trends. If the trend is negative, you might consider buying very little. If the trend is positive, you can continue trading.

Technical Analysis: It studies the supply and demand of stock within the market. There are five variables to consider strongly. They are:

1. **P/E ratio:** You calculate the price-to-earnings ratio by dividing the stock's market value per share by its earnings per share. To determine the value of a stock, investors compare a stock's P/E ratio to those of its competitors and industry standards. Lower P/E ratios are seen favorably by investors.
2. **EPS:** A company's earnings per share show how efficiently its revenue is flowing down to investors. An increasing EPS is taken as a good sign by the investors.
3. **PEG ratio:** To calculate PEG (price-to-earnings growth ratio), divide the P/E ratio by the 12-month growth rate. Investors usually consider a stock valuable if the PEG is lower than 1.
4. **Book value:** Company's price-to-book ratio is another way to determine a stock's future prospect.

Investors typically use this method to find high-growth companies that are undervalued. The formula P/B ratio equals the market price of a company's stock divided by its book value of equity. The book value of equity is derived by subtracting the book value of liabilities from the book value of assets. Investors view a low P/B ratio as a sign that the stock is potentially undervalued.

5. **ROE:** Return on equity is calculated by dividing net income by average shareholders' equity. A continual increase in ROE is a good sign to investors. Never use your money in share business, which is your monthly need. Either you invest your extra money or you take time to save money to trade. Try to gather enough knowledge before your investment, analyze the market, think wisely and then invest your capital there.

2. 15 Best Tips for Stress Management

Category: Mental health > Stress management

Summary: This article will illustrate certain approaches to handle stress in our daily life.

Body: Pressure creates stress in our life which is a common phenomenon in our existence. Sometimes it compels us to take action and move forward. But, if we get overwhelmed by stress, it might be a problem for us. Stress can affect people both physically and mentally. As time goes on, our life is getting more busy and competitive. This is why we are getting stressed more often. Stress can hamper our present effort, and our present effort will shape our future. Thus, tension and anxiety may destroy our coming times and dreams. These particular 15 ways describe how to handle stress in our life.

1. A proper diet plan is a must for stress management. Healthy foods can boost our mental health. It can minimize the effects of stress, build up our immune system, strengthen our mood, and also lower our

blood pressure. Avocado, banana, tea, fatty fish, complex carbohydrates, lean proteins, meat, eggs, nuts, beans, fruits, carrots, yogurt, berries, vegetables, spices such as ginger; all are quite beneficial for our body.

2. Doing exercise on a regular basis will definitely help us to reduce our stress. It can be in ways like dancing, swimming, running, cycling and aerobics. Walking in sunlight and also in fresh air will stimulate our mind as well as decrease anxiety and tension. Physical exercise ensures better blood circulation, which raises the oxygen level in the whole body. Thus it will help us to fight against stress successfully.

3. We have to sleep properly in a scheduled time for almost six to eight hours. It will help to remove our tiredness, refresh our brain and mind. Therefore, it will restore our minds with energy and ease. An energetic mind will be always stress-free.

4. We must avoid using electronics before going to sleep. We should stop operating our gadgets almost half an hour before bedtime. It will divert our concentration toward better sleep, and sound sleep always ensures a stronger and stress-free mind.

5. Sometimes, we should take deep breaths. They allow our body in full exchange of incoming oxygen and outgoing carbon dioxide. It helps stabilize blood pressure and also lower stress.

6. Maintaining a disciplined life will help us to have a tension-free life. If we accomplish all of our work on a timely basis and follow the daily routine

strictly, it will not create any sudden work pressure that causes stress in our life.

7. When any hard and prolonged task appears before us to complete, if we break down the whole work in different steps and start doing it step by step, it will become easier to bring to an end. In this way, people will not go through a stressful situation to finish the whole work.

8. Every work must have prior planning and preparation to be done on time. In this way, we will be able to finish our work with ease rather than in stress.

9. We must have a positive attitude. A positive mindset can solve thousands of difficulties and win hardships. Sometimes there may be some situations that we are unable to change. We have to accept that we can never change. If we cannot change the situation, then we have to change our reaction toward it. This is how we will take control over complex circumstances and keep our minds free from all kinds of stress and anxiety.

10. Self-respect and self-love also give energy to our minds. When we realize that we really love our self and respect our decisions, it gives an inner spirit in our mind and keeps us refreshed.

11. We should always spend some time only for ourselves. It will keep us away from strains and worries. We can practice our hobbies at a particular time, like spending some time gardening, painting, reading novels, and so on. It will assist us in developing a stress-free mind.

12. We must spend some time with our family, hang outs during the weekend and share our feelings with our family members. In this way, stress will be just flying away from our life.
13. Sometimes, there may be something that we would not be able to share with our family. In that case, we should talk with our friends, peers, or colleagues. It will relieve us from mental suffering.
14. We must learn to say "No." If anything is beyond our ability, we should leave that by saying no.
15. Finally, keeping a strong belief in our own religion and practicing religious activities will always keep our minds free from any kind of anxiety, distress, and tension.

I believe, above 15 tips to manage stress will help you too in your daily life.

3. Tips to Take Exam Preparations in Best Ways

Category: Education and science

Summary: I used to follow these ways to prepare myself for exams. I expect it will also work for you or your kids.

Body: Nothing comes true over the night. We have to give effort with full patience and also we have to move on step by step. If you really want to be successful in your life discipline, punctuality, hard work, and motivation; everything is important. Student life is the building period of our life. The whole life, how it will be, really depends on how we have spent our student life. It is the watering season of seed which will turn into a fruitful tree one day.

Exams may be a horrible experience for some students, but why? A student's job is to cultivate his brain through study. If he really follows proper rules and guidelines, exams will never turn into unpleasant experience in his life. There could be certain directions.

1. It is always very important to follow the class lectures and take notes. Whatever the teacher is telling during class time, every word is extremely important. The whole topic will appear very easy if any student just follows the teacher's instructions carefully. During my Bachelor's, Master's, and second Master's degree, after finishing every class, I had to wait a minimum of one hour as some students used to photocopy my class notes. Surprisingly, among them, some peers could only pass several courses just because they followed my class memorandum.

2. Just go through the topic every day after the class. It may be in the afternoon or night but make sure you are reading the subject matter regularly. If you skip even for one day, it will create a study gap. That is the reason most of the students feel helpless before the exam. Irregular study habit is a dangerous proceeding in student life.

3. Make sure your concept is totally clear. Once you have a clear idea about the subject matter, studies will become very enjoyable before you. When we start to love our studies or work, it never seems hard for us. This is a vital concern in our life to love our job (work or study). You may join in group study with friends and peers if you feel hard to understand any hypothesis. Sharing your difficulties with your classmates will make you clear about those inflexible points.

4. Never leave any home works or assignments pending. These help you to get prepared for the

final exam. Learning is a chronological process. It is never possible to learn so many things within a day. Thus, never skip any step.

5. There will be class tests or quizzes. Appear those with complete preparation. Never ignore these small exams, which will lead you to sit for weighty assessments.

6. Exam dates would always be declared before the half-yearly, midterm, or final exams. Start revising your chapters, subject matters at least one week before. The more you revise, it will increase your ability to hold ideas for a long time.

7. Be relaxed before the exam night. If you follow the above rules you don't need to be panicked just before the exam that most of the students really experience. Make your last revision, sleep well and appear the exam with a cool brain to next day.

This is how I have passed my academic journey. I hope you will also benefit from my learning philosophy. Actually, the purpose of a degree is not only to get good grades. It is all about acquiring knowledge and skill. It is to prepare yourself for practical life. It is our knowledge or wisdom that finally helps us to move forward in our life. A wise person will always be successful in his life. He will know about proper resource utilization, time management, and also embracing the struggles of life. An astute person knows if he takes a risk, it will return to him one day with a real victory.

Our student life is the path where we get the chance to develop ourselves for our future life. These exams are the assessments of how much we have learned.

Learning is easy if you follow the rules step-by-step. It will be very hard if you try to learn so many things at a time. Now it is your choice, whether you will make it feasible or inflexible!

4. Why Do I Love to Write on HubPages?

Category: Books, literature, and writing

Summary: You will know about the reasons behind my choice of writing on this website through this article.

Body: I had some likelihood of writing since my childhood. But at the same time, it was also true that I had never thought of becoming a writer in my future. My potentiality has grown with time. I used to enjoy doing my creative assignments in university. Now, I intend to write quality articles where readers will get some information, and they will also be pleased to read those. I get immense satisfaction through writing. It is another world for me. I always feel lucky to be connected with HubPages, where there are vast options to reveal our aptitude on an international platform. There are ten specific reasons for my devotion to writing on HubPages. They are:

1. HubPages gives me the chance to utilize the knowledge that I have gained from my academic degrees. As I have completed my BBA, MBA, and

also my second Master's in Applied English Language and Linguistics, I am eligible to write articles on multiple topics. This website has just opened an era where I can convey my wisdom to different readers. It seems to me how worthy my degrees really are due to HubPages.

2. Sharing our own views always benefits us. Sometimes, I feel like sharing some of my personal experiences with all hubbers, which gives me pleasure. Even it helps me to overcome my sadness as well.

3. This is a platform where I can share my unique ideas that help in expanding my potentialities. It helps to keep my brain active and also practice my intelligence. In this way, I will be able to be more precise with time.

4. As HubPages is a revenue-generating website; thus, it gives me an opportunity to make a good income by publishing quality articles. Specially featured articles attract better future opportunities.

5. There is a large number of hubbers writing on HubPages; it has a big writers' society. It creates an upstanding chance for me to know about so many topics, new ideas, and skills from others. I asked myself, "How creative could people be." I just feel amazed reading some of the articles that are just quite fantastic to go through. Eventually, it is helping me with my self-development. Now, I feel more encouraged to write and publish new articles here, which is paving my way for career opportunities in the writing world.

6. After joining HubPages, I spend my leisure time reading interesting and unique articles by different hubbers over there. In our crazy busy life, a quality pass time is essential to stimulate our minds and move on. Now, HubPages is serving me one.

7. It creates a chance to make connections with professional writers. As we know that a strong professional network can help you to make an important career move, HubPages is offering this possibility to me.

8. By publishing articles here, I am gaining more self-confidence than before to move on. Greater self-confidence allows you to get rid of self-doubt and negative thoughts about yourself. It offers a straight path with great energy to start and finish your work.

9. After getting associated with HubPages account, I got huge feasibility to know about updated information of the recent world, world economy, and business. It offers me to have a sophisticated mind that notices the contemporary details of the world.

10. HubPages awarded me with the golden opportunity to be professionally active even after having a very young kid of mine. I can read books and browse the internet to gather ideas for my selected topic from home. Also, I can type my writings and publish these from home. Therefore, I am blessed to be a proud mother who gets the chance to pursue her career by maintaining perfect motherhood due to HubPages.

Finally, whenever I publish any new article, it gives me tremendous inspiration to proceed while noticing the number of readers who read it. It gives me a feeling of self-actualization that is the realization of one's potential and the full progress of one's abilities and appreciation for life.

These are all about why I am very much passionate and excited to write and publish articles on this website called HubPages, which is just like a source of cognition, mastery and also satisfaction for me.

5. 21st Century and the Dynamic Business World

Category: Business and employment

Summary: 21st century brought about a big recast in its business portrayal. How?

Body: This is the age of e-commerce. Businesses have flourished extensively throughout the whole world in the 21st century. Demand for business graduates has increased, people are more inclined toward attaining degrees in business.

Multinationals, corporations, banks, and other financial institutions have been raised to a higher level. People are getting more opportunities everywhere to prove their talent and qualities. Life is getting busier day by day even though ease also came. People are becoming more technology-oriented rather than depending on themselves. During the 21st century, the dynamic business world has brought about a huge dramatic change in every aspect of life.

- Banks and other financial institutions are giving a loan to small businesses to encourage people toward doing some business and earning profit. Once these businesses start to earn a profit, it will create economic growth; slowly, it will increase the GDP. This is how this opportunity is helping a country as a whole to improve the world economy. These banks and financial institutions are also offering good fixed deposit rates where clients are benefitted, and these institutions keep the capital for their business for a certain period of time. Thus, both the clients and institutions are becoming profitable with time, and the country is also gaining assistance as well.

- Entrepreneurial businesses have started. People are moving ahead as entrepreneurs and having achievements. Resultants businesses, street food businesses are taking place. People are getting self-dependent with time. They are also coming with new business ideas. Different companies are collecting unique business ideas by organizing events and conducting award ceremonies. Some of those ideas are implemented in real and come to a successful point. This is how it is creating money generating sources for the society. Young stars, fresh graduates and even experienced persons are also getting involved in these kinds of activities.

- Business has reached to its maximum growth by introducing franchising, licensing, and joint ventures. International business has started taking place throughout the whole world. People are making money by investing in share markets. They go for both long and short-term investments and earn profit. Different companies offer initial public offering (IPO) to people. Public, those who understand the market wisely, are able to generate huge profit from share business. Some get the profit from long-term investment again; some get it through short-term investment, daily trading.

- Internet access has brought about significant ease and opportunities for the business world. People can communicate easily, no matter which part of the world they are in. International transactions are happening. People are promoting their products and services through social media (Facebook, Twitter, Instagram, etc.). Online businesses are popular nowadays. People are more self-dependent than before. They get the latest updates easily through social networking websites. These online businesses are getting the profile of developing countries higher than before. They are getting more options to create a better future. Customers can order easily through the internet, which is about to knock at the door within a short interval of time. People get to know about the latest fashion, current world, how everything is changing, world economy, international job market, business opportunities in different countries and how to move on within a short period of time. Client and customer relationship is getting better due to the trouble-free communication system.

- The 21st century has been introduced to social welfare, CSR (Corporate Social Responsibility); those are working for the sake of society as well as for a country as a whole. Corporate Social Responsibility is a type of business self-regulation with the aim of being socially accountable. In today's socially conscious environment, employees and customers place a premium on working for and spending their money with a business that prioritizes CSR. It benefits both the business and the society. Several companies and enterprises are donating to blind people, orphanages, and children with special needs. This is how they are creating their strong positive impression in the society which benefits both the society and the company itself by creating customer satisfaction and brand loyalty.

This is how the 21st century has blessed us with dynamic business opportunities where we are able to establish ourselves in our own way. The business world is always very challenging. But there are a variety of options for us. Our vision, smart choice, hard work, patience, and favor of this age will certainly make us successful one day.

6. Career Opportunities In Accounting

Category: Business and employment > accounting

Summary: This article will illustrate how a degree and knowledge in accounting will help you to build your career.

Body: Accounting is the process where all financial information and transactions are recorded and analyzed.

As we know that accounting plays a vital role in an organization or a company. It keeps all records of revenue, expenditure, profit, loss, inventory, assets, transactions with other companies and customers, clients, suppliers, bank loans, repayment of those loans, amount of interest, and also all other monetary actions that take place in a company or an organization. Without the accounting department, it is almost impossible to run a business. It ensures whether a business is going profitably or not. The ultimate objective of a business is to earn profit.

Therefore, without keeping exact records of all financial information and settlements, there is no meaning of doing any business at all.

As the subject and its implication in the field life are very important for any kind of business, it naturally gives us a sign about the bright career opportunities in this relevant field.

Firstly, all organizations are bound to have their accounting department where accountants and accounting graduates are needed. So, from a very generic point of view, accounting graduates have some natural market demand all over the world.

The world economy is based on businesses and different financial institutions. Without financial institutions, an economy will not be able to move on. Banks and other financial institutions provide loans against a certain interest rate. Small and large business entrepreneurs start their businesses with these loans. They got established with time by earning more profit which raises a country's GDP. Higher GDP creates a strong profile of a country before the whole world. This is how banks and financial institutions play an essential role in the economic growth of a country, and these organizations need to keep all banking and financial records very strictly to move on. As a consequence, professional accountants, certified chartered accountants, and accounting graduates all are very important to run all activities in these banks and financial institutions. All of these explained needs of work create good career opportunities for accounting students.

Secondly, any kind of other institutions like schools, colleges, universities, corporations, insurance companies, event management companies, all kinds of private, government, and semi-government institutions have the same need to keep all kinds of financial records. As a result, accounting students get more job opportunities for relevant posts, ensuring a better set of circumstances.

Thirdly, a degree and knowledge in accounting could help a person for any kind of entrepreneur start in business. He may come up with his own accounting firm. He could even manage the accounts of his own business. It gives enough confidence due to a person's knowledge in a relevant field.

Fourthly, auditing is a demanding portion of an accounting career. The internal employees do and settle all financial transactions and update them. Auditors are the external accountants who judge the reliability and verifiability of the works of internal employees. Auditors will confirm whether the companies are showing true and accurate information in their financial statements or not. Therefore, a degree and knowledge in accounting will also throw a chance of being an auditor, which offers better career options for professional graduates in accounting.

Lastly, the teaching profession also needs good accounting graduates for satisfactory performance of teaching in relevant fields. In schools, colleges and universities everywhere, there is a demand for quality accounting teachers who can deliver the best accounting knowledge to their students. Today's teachers will gift the society for tomorrow. Thus, quality accounting graduates will always be a priority in the teaching profession as well, which paves their path for more chances to build their careers.

7. Diglossia and Its Advantages, Disadvantages

Category: Linguistics

Summary: Diglossia is a term in socio-linguistics, where the same language is used in two ways in a society or community. Let us read thoroughly about the concept.

Body: When a particular speech community's people use two versions of the same language, then it is called Diglossia. If Diglossia exists in society, then that society is called Diglossic society.

There are two related terms in the concept. These are high variety and low variety. High variety (H) is used in formal situations like in literature and mass media, and low variety (L) is used in ordinary conversations. High variety is a reflection of prestige and status, whereas low variety is a reflection of common ranking.

Children learn low variety as a native language. It is the language of home, the family, the streets, and marketplaces, friendship and solidarity. By contrast, the high variety is spoken by few people. It must be taught in school. High variety is used for public speaking, formal lectures, higher education, television broadcasts, sermons, liturgies, and writing.

Advantages of Diglossia: There could be five advantages of using diglossia in a society.

1. **Introducing a social dialect:** Sometimes, the lower variety can be turned into a social dialect with time.

2. **Borrow words from other languages:** When people use lower variety, they use words from different other languages they know, or they learn from watching TV and using social media. Using randomly other words may enter into a particular language. In this way, a language borrows words from different other languages. This is how diglossia can benefit a particular language.

3. **Prestige issue:** For people who can use the high variety, it gives them a feeling of self-esteem. They feel proud to have the ability to use the high variety in society. Here, diglossia introduces a matter of social dignity among the people. People tend to learn the high variety to earn a good reputation in a certain community.

4. **Correct use of the language in high variety:** As people use the exact rule of grammar in the high variety of diglossia, it continues to use the language according to the rule among them. It focuses on accurate learning of the language in high variety. This is how diglossia enhances the opportunity to retain a language as claimed by the required rules.

Maintaining proper acts in a language helps it to exist for a long time. It lessens the probability of a language becoming extinct very easily.

5. **Enhance good quality in writing:** High variety follows accuracy in sentence construction rules regarding grammar and punctuation. It is also strict in maintaining five major components of language; phonemes, morphemes, lexemes, syntax, and context. Following all rules strengthen the quality of writing in a language automatically.

Disadvantages of Diglossia: There could be five disadvantages of using diglossia in a community.

1. **Using low variety breaks the rules of a language:** People don't use any grammatical rules while using the low variety in diglossia. Therefore, using low variety puts less importance on the grammatical issue. It slowdowns the language acquisition process as rules are not applied properly.

2. **Change the habit:** In low variety, people use slang. As they use low variety among friends and family, it may become their habit to use slang always. Therefore, they may forget the origin of their language and its real sentence construction rules as well. This may be a threat for the language to exist in the long run before the world.

3. **Introduce discrimination:** Some people in a society have no idea about the high variety of diglossia. Therefore, high variety using people may underestimate the people using low variety of

diglossia as there is a status issue for people using high variety.

4. **Threaten the existence of a language:** Using low variety diglossia creates vulnerability in a language. Uncertainty arises concerning the existence of the language.

5. **Its impact on teaching and learning:** Usually, students are habituated to use low variety in family and friends. When teachers use high variety while delivering their lectures, students have difficulty understanding it. That is why sometimes they understand the class content less due to low variety diglossia.

Diglossic conditions, situations, and their impact may vary from country to country over different languages for different contexts.

8. The Academic, Cultural and Global Effects of Bilingual Education System

Category: Linguistics

Summary: This twenty-first century is the best time for globalization which is really bringing the whole world very close. The bilingual education system has made a huge contribution in bringing the world almost into our hands as it is helping in communication by using English as a first or second language over the world. Let us know about the blessings of this education system.

Body: In a Bilingual Education system, the teacher teaches students using two languages—both native and second language. There could be several reasons along with advantages to using a bilingual education system in different educational institutions over the world. There is no doubt about the superiority of this education system. The three supreme effects are described below:

1. **Academic effect:** Children learn their native language from a very early stage of their life. It becomes easy for them to acquire knowledge in their native language. Every child's upbringing is surrounded by his mother language. English is the second language for countries where they have their different domestic language apart from English. It is the global language. Therefore, the medium of instruction of most universities over the world is English.

Even though English is an international language, still sometimes it becomes an important issue to use the native language in the classroom. Especially when it is time to teach younger students, using a native language becomes necessary as they need more help with their native language. Here, teachers can use both English and the domestic language to make their understanding clear. The purpose of education is to convey knowledge to the learners. Therefore, using both languages is helping students to gain their required knowledge, which becomes a blessing of this education system.

A bilingual education system encourages students to learn, helps them to practice their intelligence. They start to learn mastery regarding both of the languages from their early childhood. It enhances their creativity and interest to grasp more. It also makes them smart and creates good future opportunities as well. Their working memory improves day by day due to studying two languages at a time. They get adept at using two languages, which is a great achievement in their whole academic journey.

Even in the case of graduating students, the bilingual education system really assists them. Sometimes, several hard and controversial topics are presented before the students to learn. It appears really difficult for the teachers to make them understand without the help of the mother language. This is how the bilingual education system is helping both students and teachers from all aspects.

2. **Cultural effect:** The bilingual education system has a strong cultural effect. Immigrants get the chance to learn the particular country's indigenous language. As they develop an understanding of that new language, they also start to learn about the new culture. They get in contact with those people and their language. This is how the use of the native language brings immigrants closer to native people and helps them learn about their social norms and values. In this way, the bilingual education system can transfer the native culture to immigrants. For example, if a Spanish family becomes an immigrant in Germany where the first language is German. The kids will go to school, and due to the bilingual education system, they will learn German language in their educational institution. Slowly, it will help them acknowledge the German culture as they will start to learn the local language. This is the native language (German) which will be helping them to acquire German culture with time.

The bilingual education system has its strong socio-cultural effect. One culture is transferring to another culture through this. The world is getting more attached from country to country through this education system. There is more cultural mixing now. People are exploring the world more than before. They are working together, exchanging their views among different countries and acquiring different traditions as well. Exploring different lifestyles, people are becoming broad-minded, opening the doors of their minds and flying like birds in the endless blue sky.

3. **Global effect:** Bilingualism introduced globalization and harmony among the universe. It provides a multidimensional view of language learning that contains five categories; individual, societal, family, school, and disciplinary. It encourages each group of students to work together in learning each other's language. It is helping to connect people globally.

The goal of the bilingual education system is to teach students using two languages—both native and second language. Bilingual individuals have the ability to switch between two languages. It is creating cognitive control among the students. Students are becoming wizards using both languages simultaneously. Sometimes they disengage from one language and engage in the other language.

9. Twelve Best Ways to Win Depression

Category: Mental health

Summary: Nowadays, depression is a common issue in people's life. It hampers our regular living. Therefore, it is important to know about this psychological problem and how to get rid of this for our better survival. I hope these twelve tips will really work out and help us to move toward becoming better people.

Body: Sometimes depression affects our life. It is a very common issue in people's life. People may even commit suicide due to depression. Therefore, it is really important to rid ourselves of it. Depression affects our work, daily life, and also relationships. It may be caused due to various kinds of reasons like family, relationships, and also from study-related issues. There could also be career and financial issues. It is a very prime concern to know how to win against depression for a healthy life.

There are twelve effective ways to get rid of depression.

1. **Avoid overthinking:** Sometimes, we overthink about our exam results, career, and future which may put us down. This thinking slows down our works and puts stress on our brain. Consequently, the effectiveness of our work becomes less. This kind of issue may create depression in our minds. We have to give our full effort, leaving all kinds of over thinking. It will help us enhance productivity, keep our minds out of depression as well.

2. **Utilize every moment of life:** Time and tide wait for none. Keeping ourselves busy with work will give us no chance of unnecessary thinking. Our brain and body will be active, which will create good blood circulation. Blood flow increases in people who are not depressed. This is how being active in all aspects of our life will help us remove the downturn from our life.

3. **Routine bound life:** A person must complete his daily life activities under a certain routine. A routine-bound life helps us finish our work on time, keeps our mind stress free along with improving our mental health as well. A stress-free mind will hardly fall into depression.

4. **Maintain perfect hours for sleeping:** Adult persons have to sleep about eight hours at night to maintain good health. A major cause of depression could be less sleep at night. At the same time, we should wake up early morning in order to have a fresh mind which can win against gloominess easily.

5. **Regular physical exercise:** Physical exercise provides more oxygen to our brain, which helps the growth of brain cells. A strong brain has the power to overcome any kind of depression quickly.

6. **Religious activities:** Practicing religious activities on a regular basis give spirit to our mind. It also gives us stimulation in our daily life. A stimulated mind is strong enough to handle the stresses of life and move on. People get their inner peace in their religious beliefs. A peaceful soul can get rid of stagnation by itself.

7. **Make parents happy:** Parents are the best buddies, shelter, and place of eternal love to every person in the world. Their support makes us successful and gives us peace. We can share any of our feelings with them, and they are the people who will do their best to rescue us from any kind of sadness or danger. If people try to make their parents happy, it really gives immense pleasure to them as there is nothing better than their blessings in our life. Their blessings and support give us the mental strength to fight any kind of hard situation in life. Depression will just fly away with their brace.

8. **Ignore unnecessary comments of other people:** People may have their own opinions on our way of life. It's important for us to take good advice and to ignore the rubbish ones. Listening to all opinions will make us depressed as we have only one goal in our life. In order to be successful, it is important to have a stress free-mind where there is no prominent sadness and depression.

9. **Love your work:** We have to love our works. If we don't love our work, it's just a wastage of our time. Passion and love toward our work and job will never let depression even touch our minds.

10. **Travel as much as possible:** Travelling to different places really refreshes our minds from monotonous and boring life. It gives us energy and makes our minds enthusiastic. Enjoying natural beauty helps us to remove misery from our life. People should travel at least twice a year according to their affordability. It may be within the country. Again they can fly to another country as well. It helps to meet different people around the world. People get chances to observe others' lifestyle, their ease, and also hardship as well. They can share their feelings if it really matches. The warm feeling of traveling offers people a greater heart full of love and happiness.

11. **Practice hobby in leisure:** People have different kinds of hobbies like; reading storybooks, listening to music, watching movies, going for a long drive, gardening and so on. No matter which one is our hobby exactly, we should practice it in our leisure time for a sound mind. Our hobbies help us to utilize our leisure time properly. It helps to improve our mental soundness. Research shows that people with hobbies are less likely to suffer from stress, low mood, and depression. These activities make us feel happier and more relaxed.

12. **Keep in touch with good friends and well-wishers:** We have to be connected with good

friends who are really our well-wishers. If we share the issues regarding our despair with them, they will give us good advice and will help us to come out of it. The person himself will be relaxed after sharing his feelings with a right-minded friend.

Following the above tips, I strongly believe that any person can win against depression which is a common problem nowadays among people over the whole world.

10. Impact of Wages on Employee Productivity

Category: Business and employment

Summary: This discussion will let you know how employees get motivated by getting their proper remuneration.

Body: The world changed with time. Once, it was an agro-based economy. Industrialization started in the 18th century in Britain. Then it spread over the world. Our 21st century is an industry-based world where massive economic growth is happening. There are five factors of industrialization (land, labor, capital, technology, and connections). Employees give labor in return for wages which is a crucial concept in the industry. Owners always want to exploit the employees. There is always a management conflict between the top level and employees in an organization. The employees deserve the proper earnings according to their level, post, and hard work. At the same time, owners also want to reduce the cost of the company. Keeping in a balanced position, possessors have to determine the proper wages of employees as it influences the productivity as well as all-over growth of an industry. Six particular descriptions are given below:

1. There is no doubt that the distribution of wages in a deserved manner will enhance the quality of the workers. Once they start getting proper remuneration, their motivation will boost, which will increase the standard of their work. If the employees are underpaid, it decreases the acceleration of their work very naturally. The company is going to suffer in the long run indeed. There is no substitution for quality work in this world. If there is no quality, there will be no expected outcome as well.

2. Employee satisfaction is a very important issue for an organization. Satisfied employees give their best to the company, which leads it toward success. Employee satisfaction depicts whether the employees are happy and are able to fulfill their desired needs. Employee satisfaction depends on different things. Among them, wage is very basic.

3. Often, we have heard about the strikes that employees start in an organization. Employees initiate riots, work stoppages when they feel that they are getting underpaid, deprived of deserved benefits and they may also have the question of job security in their mind. Every country has its individual labor laws; under that, owners cannot exploit human labor, and they have to provide all privileges and rights the employees are worthy of. This kind of strike hampers the flow of work in a

company that automatically reduces production. Sometimes, it becomes very hard for the owner to bring control again. Therefore, it is always better to ensure the correct fixation of salaries according to country law so that employees will not think of doing any mass to the company.

4. Experienced workers working in a company for a long time are the assets of the company. They are highly productive for the company. If they get a better package outside, they will definitely switch. This kind of switch is a great loss for an organization. Thus, the owner needs to be always careful about the market rate of salary for different positions and should provide it accordingly. In some cases, they should provide more than others to hold the employees for the long run. This policy will help for employee retention, and employee retention always enhances the company's yield.

5. Disbursement of handsome payments to workers creates a good reputation for any company. Due to word-of-mouth communication, these topics spread easily from person to person. More skilled personnel get interested to work for a good salary. Therefore, when the time for any recruitment comes, the required board gets a chance to hire efficient employees for the company, which is also related to a company's productivity. Qualified workers are more eligible to carry on their responsibility in a perfect way.

6. The impact of wages controls overall organizational growth. There are four stages of

growth (startup, growth, maturity, renewal). Human resource is very important for each stage to carry on. Human resource (employees) will only function at their best effort once they get the acceptable honorarium.

From the above discussion, it is pretty clear about the impact of wages on employee productivity. Employees are the main asset of an organization. They always try hard to achieve the organizational goals to reach the desired success. Their contribution is beyond any clarification. Thus, taking care of them by providing excellent remuneration is always required. This is how an organization will move toward real victory.

11. CSR Benefits both the Business and a Society. How?

Category: Business and society

Summary: When businesses are walking extra miles to generate a profit, they also do good to the environment and society. This is how CSR works.

Body: Corporate Social Responsibility is a type of business self-regulation with the aim of being socially accountable. There is no one 'right' way companies can practice CSR; many corporate CSR initiatives strive to positively contribute to the public, the economy, or the environment. In today's socially conscious environment, employees and customers place a premium on working for and spending their money with a business that prioritizes CSR.

CSR benefits both the business and the society. The business can be benefitted in eight ways.

1. CSR brings better brand recognition. Brand recognition is the ability of a consumer to recognize one brand over other brands. When a company is

contributing toward social welfare, it usually promotes the contribution in newspapers, journals, TV channels, and also social media. People become able to recognize a certain brand fast. It creates better brand acknowledgment in the market for the company.

2. CSR creates a strong business reputation. Once a company is doing for the well-being of a society, it attracts large numbers of people toward its business. The importance of a good reputation in business is just beyond any explanation. Without a good reputation, no business can run for a long time. It will also fail to generate profit. A company's superiority in the market largely depends on its reputation. Good reputations will always attract loyal customers, which is a great beneficial acquisition for a company.

3. CSR helps to increase sales and customer loyalty. As people get good apprehensions through CSR, the company's sales automatically increase, which generates more profit as well. It also creates customer loyalty due to their societal devotion. Loyal customers are not willing to switch their preferences to other brands very easily. CSR will help produce constant, faithful, and resolute customers who will help a company to live in a tough competition.

4. The expenses incurred due to CSR can be considered under operational cost. Operational costs are the costs of resources used by an organization just to maintain its existence.

Therefore, cost due to CSR is included in a company's operational cost. Thus, companies will not feel that CSR is very expensive. This is how considering CSR cost separately naturally reduces a company's operational cost.

5. CSR enhances financial performance. It creates a good image before the stakeholders, which favors a company in all aspects.

    From internal stakeholders, employees and managers will give their best performance to their work due to the strong notion of the company. From external stakeholders, suppliers will be always in favor. Society, government, and creditors will be on the company's side. Shareholders will buy more shares. Last but not least, customers will be trusted customers.

6. CSR will increase the ability to attract talent and retain staff. As CSR works for social welfare, people working in other companies get to know about it. Sometimes, they may switch to a strong company due to their talent. This is how CSR attracts more efficient employees toward the company. It also helps in staff retention. Developing strong CSR helps companies create a strong brand identity. Usually, employees have little tendencies to switch from a well-built company.

7. CSR increases organizational growth. Being a socially responsible company can bolster a company's image and build its brand. Social responsibility empowers employees to leverage the

corporate resources at their disposal for good. Former CSR programs can boost employee morale and lead to greater productivity in the workforce.

8. The better a firm's performance, the fewer capital restraints it will face. Better CSR performance helps earn improved stakeholder engagement which pushes managers to adopt a long-term strategy. Long-term strategies help a business by allowing it to be proactive in its growth rather than by simply reacting to market conditions.

A society benefit from CSR in five ways.

1. Companies may hold charity for orphans, special needs children, and old people. This is great support for a society with this kind of people who need help to survive.

2. Restaurant owners sometimes feed street kids in a particular area. This is also a beneficiary part of executing CSR for a society. CSR also works for improving labor policies. It helps ensure labor rights in a community.

3. Companies also donate to ensure a clean environment for the country. Dust removal programs and tree plantation projects really ensure a better environment for the society, which helps maintain a good ecological balance in the earth as well.

4. Companies arrange different kinds of social awareness programs under CSR, which make people aware of different cardinal issues in society.

5. Finally, CSR works for the society, which develops a country's overall situation. Slowly, it helps to increase patriotism among people, which benefits the country as a whole.

To conclude, CSR should be inbuilt into the functioning of various activities of the corporate sector. It should be a way of life for them due to its benefits to the society and the business world as well as the country on the whole.

12. Challenges of Succession Planning

Category: Human Resources (HR)

Summary: There are several challenges to overcome to ensure successful succession planning.

Body: Succession planning is a concept where a company has a plan for a future leader if it appears the question of replacement. It could be for any reason; the person may leave or may pass away. Any unpredictable situation may happen. Therefore, every company must have their succession planning so that they don't fall into dangerous or uncertain situations in the future. It is also known as 'Replacement Planning.'

Basically, succession planning is both strategic and an economic necessity. A business has versatile domains to consider and accept challenges to move on. This succession planning is also a very challenging issue as replacing a leader is not a matter of joke. There are so many challenges to consider. Each one is described below:

1. While brainstorming with succession planning, the HR department could be biased to promote some person. Biasness is human nature. It comes automatically, no matter how professional a person is. It is a challenge to overcome bigotry by maintaining exact rationale while preparing the succession plan for a company.

2. Sometimes HR department delays in preparing the succession planning. As a consequence, when it becomes urgent to replace any personnel, they do hurry for selection. In this way, sometimes proper evaluation is not done and the right person is not placed at the right position at the right time. It hampers a company's regular functions and defers the activities as well.

3. Succession planning for a big company or enterprise is really very challenging. There would be lots of selection processes for different departments. If the rules and guidelines are not properly followed, it creates a misleading decision which brings about a dangerous effect for the company in future.

4. Sometimes, poor communication with all departments and employees creates a problem. All individuals, departments, and employees should be aware of this planning. If they are not aware of this policy, they may react with any sudden implication of prior planning.

5. Once in a while, seniors may have some tendencies to dominate others. This is a big challenge regarding the issue. In some cases, succession

planning may fail to be executed in an appropriate way due to seniors' influential power.

6. Sometimes past performance records may not be enough to judge any personnel for a higher position or post. If there is a departmental shift toward a better position, HR needs to qualify the competencies more strictly so that the person would able to understand and finish his responsibilities in an efficient and effective way.

7. Succession planning needs to be updated or reviewed at least twice a year. It is a dynamic process; lacking proper renovated information and employee performance will hinder the required promotional process. If the right person is not selected for the right place, the company will suffer in the long run.

8. Sometimes, there could be some shortcomings in strategies of succession planning. An ideal strategic plan and a course of measures could be formulated to achieve the desired goal.

9. In some cases, the roles in the succession plans are not well defined. It is a major challenge for the concern. If respected persons don't know what their duties and responsibilities are, it results in a succession plan that is little connected to the overall organization's positive output and growth.

10. Even though succession planning is under the HRM department, still it is also a part of the company as a whole. If there is no correlation between the HR department and the company's Board of Directors, senior managers, and other functional areas, then

there would be every chance for the succession planning to fail. Thus, a strong correlation among the particular departments of companies is also a big challenge for the above-discussed concern.

This business world is always very challenging. We have to compete every moment in order to survive. Succession planning is a critical concept in HRM. The HR department, along with the whole company, has to work on a regular basis to reach the maximum success that might be possible. Perhaps it may be very hard to overcome all of the challenges described above, but 100% effort can ensure the best results. Finally, having very weighted consequences of effective succession planning, every organization and business enterprise should try their best to deal with the summons, which will ensure a better future for the company as a whole.

13. Pros and Cons of Franchising Business

Category: Business and employment

Summary: Franchising is a marketing concept having its advantages and disadvantages too. Let us take a brief look.

Body: Franchising is a class of business where the owner of a particular business allows other individuals or groups to run that business (may be a product or service) upon particular terms and conditions. There is a legal contract between the two parties. The owner is called franchisor, and that individual or group is called franchisee.

The five major types of franchises are job franchise, business format franchise, product or distribution franchise, investment franchise, and conversion franchise. Dunkin' Donuts, Taco Bell, McDonald's, Sonic Drive-In, Ace Hardware, Planet Fitness, The UPS Store, KFC, Marriott International, Pizza Hut, etc., are examples of some franchises.

Advantages of franchising business: Advantages are from both sides (franchisee and franchisor).

1. The franchisor gets a great chance to expand its business worldwide. It helps with marketing and promotion. It becomes a great source of earning revenue. The franchisor only sells the brand name upon some terms and conditions. They don't need to incur any cost. They have to supervise strictly in order to maintain and ensure the perfect quality and standard of their particular product and service.

2. On the other hand, the franchisee gets an opportunity to start a business that is already established. One that already has its brand name and brand value. They just need to carry on the regular activities in order to survive in the competition.

3. The franchisee gets the chance to know about business techniques and some secrets of that particular business which may help them in their future as well.

4. As the franchisor always supervises the franchisee's activities, it ensures effective and motivated management. Ultimately, this will bring total success for the franchisee.

5. The franchisee will have limited risks and liabilities due to strict regulation of the franchisor.

6. The franchisee may not need to have a lot of experience in business as he will follow the directions of the franchisor. As we know, without having enough knowledge of business, it is always

very hard to continue. Here comes the most beneficial part of the franchisee as he can run only with the franchisor's governance.

7. The franchisee doesn't need to go for lots of marketing and promotion in its own country or territory as the brand name is already set up. It saves the cost for the franchisee. It is always a very positive side for a business if it is able to reduce its cost.

8. The franchisor needs to invest less on capital as the franchisee will pay to open each franchise. It is a great advantage for the franchisor.

9. As the franchisee is bound to maintain the stated quality and standard, it will create more customer satisfaction which will bring more brand loyal customers as well.

10. The franchisor becomes more profitable by taking royalty (money paid to the franchisor by their franchisees).

Disadvantages of franchising business: Disadvantages are also from both sides (franchisee and franchisor).

1. Firstly, there might be risk from the side of the franchisor. If the franchisee doesn't follow the proper guideline and fail to ensure the exact quality, then it will destroy the reputation of the franchisor.

2. Sometimes the location of the outlets may not be set down properly. In that case, the franchisee will not be able to generate the expected profit and may

even fail to pay the royalty to the franchisor. Eventually, if it has to shift the location or cancel the agreement, it will result in a loss for both parties.

3. It is always expensive for the franchisee as it has to bear the cost of outlet and also has to pay the franchisee's dues.

4. As the franchisee would always work upon the franchisor's direction thus, there will be less creativity from the franchisee's venture. The franchisee will always be dependent on the franchisor. It will discourage a franchisee from starting a new business on its own in the future. This is how a franchisee's potentiality will decrease with time.

5. The franchisee has to work under restrictions specified by the franchisor. There is a lack of freedom for the franchisee's side. It may create boredom in the work with time. Again, there is less privacy in work of the franchisee. It is bound to give all updates to the franchisor about everything going on in their outlet.

This dynamic business world offers us variety of options to generate money and update our lifestyle. It is up to us in which way we move. Despite having some cons, franchising business still is working as a great concept, and it has immense contribution in the world economy.

Printed in the USA
CPSIA information can be obtained
at www.ICGtesting.com
LVHW060431041023
759780LV00015B/254